American Government

FOUNDATIONS

Perritano

SADDLEBACK
EDUCATIONAL PUBLISHING

SADDLEBACK HANDBOOK SERIES

AMERICAN GOVERNMENT

Foundations

Office of the President

Congress

Supreme Court

Political Parties

Photo credits: page 17: Alamy.com; page 45: Sean Pavone/Shutterstock.com; page 48: Alamy.com; page 49: Everett Historical/Shutterstock.com; pages 50/51: Action Sports Photography / Shutterstock.com; page 60/61: Rena Schild / Shutterstock.com; page 63: Alamy.com; page 71: Alamy.com; all other images from Shutterstock.com

SADDLEBACK
EDUCATIONAL PUBLISHING
www.sdlback.com

ISBN-13: 978-1-68021-118-4
ISBN-10: 1-68021-118-8
eBook: 978-1-63078-433-1

Printed in Guangzhou, China
NOR/0116/CA21600021

20 19 18 17 16 1 2 3 4 5

TABLE OF CONTENTS

Introduction

Primary Sources

IN CO

We the People

domestic Tranquility, provide for the common defe
Posterity, All ordain and establish this Constitution

Article. I.

Introduction

Our Constitution was written in less than 100 working days. It was signed on September 17, 1787. Nine states agreed by June 21, 1788. The Constitution would be the law of the land. Then certain freedoms were guaranteed. Those were in the Bill of Rights. The other three states said yes. It was 1791.

The Constitution says what the government can do. It also says what it can't do. Most of the power is with the states. Local laws touch our lives every day.

Did the Constitution talk about teens? Give them rights? No. Teens were just property. Their parents "owned" them. What if teens broke the law? They were treated the same as adults. This upset people.

States set up courts just for teens. Called juvenile courts. Illinois was first in 1899. They saw that teens had different needs. Courts wanted to help them. But judges still had too much power. Teens were jailed without lawyers. They couldn't call their parents. The police asked questions. They had to answer. Teens didn't have the right to stay quiet. This is called self-incrimination. It is a Fifth Amendment right.

It was 1967. The Supreme Court made a ruling. It said teens had rights. These rights were protected. The Constitution said so. Teens had the right to a lawyer. And the right to stay quiet. Since then, the court has ruled many times on teen issues.

Teens have some rights to free speech at school. But not the right to disturb the class. Public schools can limit this freedom. Students can't write whatever they want in the school newspaper. Again, it's up to the school.

Teens have privacy rights at school. To a point. Their things can be searched. An adult must suspect that a rule has been broken. Rights are limited.

Especially for students in school sports. Drug testing was ruled okay. It is constitutional.

It's smart to know your rights. Important. As an engaged citizen, you also have responsibilities. Read the U.S. Constitution. It's a rulebook for our nation. People are in charge. Not the government.

The people of these United States are the rightful masters of both congresses and courts, not to overthrow the Constitution, but to overthrow the men who pervert the Constitution.
—Abraham Lincoln

Chapter 1
A NATION IN TROUBLE

It was 1783. George Washington wanted to rest. He helped win the Revolutionary War. Washington helped create the United States. Now it was time to return home to Mount Vernon, Virginia.

America was in trouble in early 1787. Each state acted like its own country. There was no president. The judicial branch didn't exist. No one made sure laws were fair. The government was broke. States could collect taxes. The federal government could not. Congress had to ask states for money. They often refused to pay.

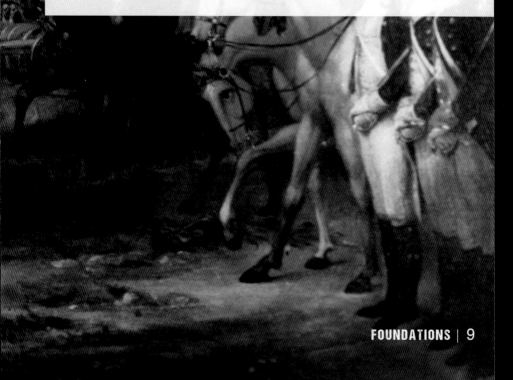

Washington's rest was short. The new nation needed him. The great general came to Philadelphia. Others also made the trip. They came to rewrite the Articles of Confederation. They were a set of laws that formed the U.S. government. By 1781, all 13 states had approved the Articles. They were the first American constitution.

Think About It: *Were the Articles of Confederation America's first fail?*

[WHAT IS A CONSTITUTION?]

A constitution is a document. It is a set of rules. Words are written down. They say how the government will work. A constitution is the starting point. It says what the government can do. And what it cannot do. It also says how much power the government will have. A constitution explains how the government is organized. Good constitutions can be changed. Why? Because people's beliefs change over time.

The first U.S. constitution was called the Articles of Confederation. States stayed independent. The central government had limited power. American leaders didn't want to create a strong central government. They had seen what too much 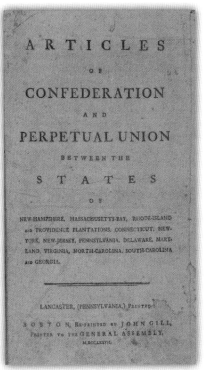 power could do. The cruelty of British rule was fresh in their minds. Plus, Americans were more loyal to their state than their country.

The Articles kept the states united. It was during the Revolutionary War. After the war the nation grew. Some people moved west. More came to the 13 states. Problems were harder to solve. The nation was too big. Our first constitution was too simple.

[MANY PROBLEMS]

The Articles were weak. States had power. But the federal government did not. Citizens were okay with that. Americans did not trust government. They had spent years under British control. King George III had taken away their freedoms. America was now its own country. The people ruled, not kings.

The Articles made problems. The government could not collect taxes. It could not set up courts.

Laws were not enforced. And the government did not have the power to control trade. There was no national army to protect the new nation.

The states were not united. Each had its own money. States collected their own taxes. Each had its own trade rules. States fought. No one had power to settle the fights.

There was no shared currency. Each state had its own. States did not look out for the good of all people. Some people went broke. The states had to come together. Or the U.S. would fail as a new nation.

[NEW RULES]

The men met at the Pennsylvania State House. Now called Independence Hall. Washington and the other men closed the doors. They shut the windows. Whatever they talked about would be a secret. The men made a decision. The Articles would not be fixed. They would be thrown away. New laws would be written. There would be a new government. This one would have greater power over the states.

HISTORY HAPPENED HERE

Event: Shays's Rebellion

Where: Massachusetts

When: Winter of 1786–1787

Farmers were broke. They couldn't pay their taxes. Many lost their land. They didn't trust state leaders. Daniel Shays wanted to help. He led protests against the courts. The farmers shut them down. Then they headed to Springfield. The government had guns there. The rebels wanted them.

State soldiers stopped them. Shays fled. The rebellion worried many. It showed the federal government's weakness. The event made leaders rethink the Articles of Confederation.

[MISTRUST]

Fixing the country was not going to be easy. Everyone had an idea. Like James Madison. He lived in Virginia. Madison wanted a strong central government. He proposed three branches of government. Legislative. Executive. And judicial.

Their powers would be separate. This was to stop abuse. Each branch would have its own job. They could not do the jobs of another branch.

Madison wanted a **bicameral** Congress. It would have two groups of lawmakers. A lower house and an upper house. The people would choose the lower house. And the lower house would choose the upper house. States with a larger population would have more power. This was because they would have more lawmakers.

The plan caused arguments. Small states did not trust big states. They wanted an equal say in government. The small states did not want to be bullied. Virginia had the largest population. Delaware, the smallest.

The men talked about other plans. Nothing worked. Things got heated. Fights broke out. Outside, people waited for news.

[SHERMAN TO THE RESCUE]

The 55 men kept at it. They were called **delegates**. Their states selected them. The men were educated. And patriotic. Twelve of the 13 states were represented. Rhode Island skipped the meeting. The work was hard. It took many hours. Everyone believed a government's power came from the people. People also had certain rights. Rights no one could take away.

Roger Sherman saved the day. He lived in Connecticut. Sherman agreed Congress should have two houses. But they would have equal power. One was the Senate. The other was the House of Representatives. Each state would have the same number of members in the Senate. But their population would decide their numbers in the House.

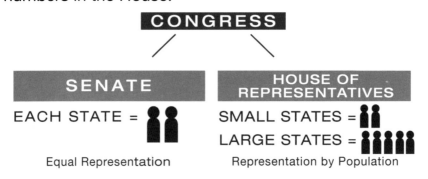

CONGRESS

SENATE
EACH STATE =
Equal Representation

HOUSE OF REPRESENTATIVES
SMALL STATES =
LARGE STATES =
Representation by Population

Sherman needed support. He wanted slave states to agree. Sherman and another delegate had a plan. Slaves should count as three-fifths of a person. Slaves at the time were "property," not people.

Tempers rose. Emotions were high. Washington listened. He kept the peace. Sherman's plan passed. The makeup of Congress was settled. Figuring out the rest of the document was easy.

The African slave trade went on until 1808. The U.S. slave trade continued. It separated families. Millions of African Americans suffered. Their lives were hard. It would be nearly 100 years before they were free. The Civil War saw to that. The Union won. The 13th Amendment was passed. Slavery was over.

["A REPUBLIC, MADAM"]

The delegates worked hard. They wrote a new set of rules. A constitution. This was the plan on how the nation would work. It had seven parts. Articles. The delegates set up three branches of government. Each had a specific job. Congress would make laws. The executive would carry them out. The judiciary would **interpret** them.

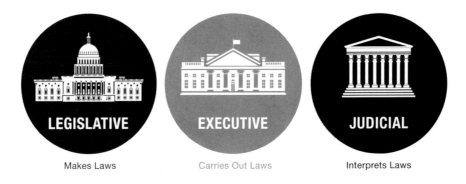

| LEGISLATIVE | EXECUTIVE | JUDICIAL |
| Makes Laws | Carries Out Laws | Interprets Laws |

Delegates knew about the dangers of cruel leaders. Too much power was bad. So they set up checks and balances. Each branch would keep an eye on the other.

These were crazy ideas. No nation had ever done these things before. America was now a democratic society. But it wasn't a **direct democracy**. Not everyone voted on all laws. It was a **constitutional representative democracy**. Ruled by laws. With elected officials who made the decisions.

The delegates finished. They walked outside. "What have you given us?" a woman yelled. "A republic, Madam," Benjamin Franklin said, "if you can keep it."

We the People
Article

Chapter 2
POWER TO THE PEOPLE

Writing new rules was easy. Getting people to agree on them was hard. George Washington left Philadelphia. So did the others. Talk did not end. Nine out of the 13 states had to okay the Constitution. They had to **ratify** it.

People debated back home. They talked in taverns and on street corners. Most were afraid. A strong government was scary. They thought it would have too much power. People had to be won over. The job fell to Alexander Hamilton, James Madison, and John Jay. They wrote the *Federalist Papers*. They were letters. Each gave reasons why people should support the Constitution. People read them.

The **Anti-Federalists** did not like the Constitution. They didn't want a strong federal government. One with more power than the states. They also wrote letters. They protested. Mobs burned copies of the document. Fights broke out.

Some states approved the Constitution. Others did not. They had to be convinced.

James Madison had the answer. Add a bill of rights, he said. Promise certain freedoms. Freedoms the government could never take away. It was a good idea. Congress added the Bill of Rights. It was 1789. All the states agreed by 1791. The nation was now united.

Think About It: *Is a direct democracy a good idea?*

[THE U.S. CONSTITUTION]

The Constitution has seven articles. Each deals with different rules. The first sets up the rules for Congress. There is also an introduction. Called the preamble. It outlines why new rules were needed.

"We the People of the United States, in Order to form a more perfect Union ..." is how it begins.

The Constitution allows for changes. This rule was set up in Article V. Congress can ask for a change. An amendment. A two-thirds vote is needed. Or two-thirds of the states can call a meeting. Then they can suggest a change. Amendments can be added. But three-fourths of the states must agree. This is not easy.

The first ten amendments to the Constitution are known as the Bill of Rights. Why does the U.S. have a Bill of Rights? People have natural rights. They can say what they want. Write what they want. Go to any church. Or not go at all. The Bill of Rights protects those and other freedoms. The government can never take them away.

The 26th Amendment changed the voting age to 18. It used to be 21. This was in 1971. Currently there are 27 amendments.

[POWER SHARING]

The U.S. is a constitutional representative democracy. We have a constitution. The people elect lawmakers. They take care of making laws. It is also a **federal republic**. We have a federal system of government. The government shares power with the states. The federal government is the boss. Most of the time. States must follow its laws. The U.S. is also a republic. We have a leader, the president.

States also make laws. And they enforce them. States set up courts just like the federal government. But states have more control over daily life.

Welcome to Texas

DRIVE FRIENDLY - THE TEXAS WAY

Each state has its own rules. They may have their own sales tax. States issue driver's licenses. Many also have income tax. This tax is paid in addition to the federal income tax.

State and federal officials often help each other. People sick with Ebola came to the U.S. in 2014. Ebola is a deadly illness. It killed many people in West Africa. The U.S. Centers for Disease Control and Prevention (CDC) set up rules. The CDC said healthcare workers should be careful. Make sure they weren't sick. Stay away from large crowds. The workers were coming home to the U.S. They had gone to Africa to help. The CDC asked states to watch the workers. Make sure they did not have Ebola.

Some states made up their own rules. They ignored the CDC's. Other states followed the CDC's advice. This is how our government works. Sometimes the states get to decide.

[SEPARATE AND EQUAL]

Each government branch has power they share. It is Congress's job to make laws. Some of its powers are specific. They are named in the Constitution. Some powers are **implied**. Congress gives itself these powers.

SPECIFIC POWERS	IMPLIED POWERS
• Borrow money • Collect taxes • Declare war • Print money • Regulate trade • Support an army and navy	• Draft people into the military • Set a federal minimum wage • Set up a national bank

The president also has many jobs. Making sure everyone follows the law is one. The president is commander in chief. This means the top military leader in the nation. Key staff is chosen by the president. The president also helps Congress make laws.

The government is big. Four million people work for it. There is a cabinet. They are the

people in charge of
15 departments. One
is the Department of
the Treasury. It prints
money. And collects
taxes. Another is the

Department of Defense. It runs the military. Each department keeps the government working. The president is the big boss.

The vice president (VP) also helps the president. The VP has to be ready to become president. This can only happen if the president dies, quits, or gets very sick. The VP's other job is president of the Senate. When there is a tie in the Senate, the VP can vote to break it.

The U.S. also has a court system. The Supreme Court is the top court. It decides when laws break a rule in the Constitution. The court calls those laws unconstitutional. Justices sit on the Supreme Court for life. Below them is the court of appeals. It looks at the rulings of lower courts. District courts are trial courts. It hears criminal and civil cases.

[CHECKS AND BALANCES]

The authors of the Constitution were smart. They wanted each branch to share power. One branch could not control another. Their idea was checks and balances. Each branch had a way to limit the power of another. There are a few ways to do this.

For example, presidents pick judges. Congress can reject them. The Supreme Court can strike down a law. Congress can undo the ruling. It can rewrite the law. Courts can convict a person of a crime. The president can **pardon** them. Congress can make a law. The president can veto it. A **veto** is when the president says no to a bill. The bill can't be a law. Two-thirds of Congress must agree to overturn a veto.

In 2015, Congress approved a natural gas pipeline. President Obama didn't like it. He wanted to protect the environment. The president vetoed the bill. Congress tried to go around him. It needed two-thirds of its members to say no to the veto. It couldn't get the votes. The pipeline bill died.

→ HISTORY HAPPENED HERE

Event: Treaty of Versailles

Who: Woodrow Wilson

When: June 28, 1919

Presidents often can't get what they want from Congress. World War I was bloody. Germany helped start the war. It was 1914. It fought against France, England, and the U.S. Germany lost four years later. It was time for peace. People wanted a peace treaty.

President Woodrow Wilson went to Paris. He fought hard for the treaty. He got what he wanted. But there was a catch. The Senate had to give its okay. It did not. Wilson was mad. He couldn't do a thing. The U.S. did not sign it. Other countries did.

Chapter 3
CIVIL RIGHTS AND CIVIL LIBERTIES

Samantha Elauf was 17. She wanted a job. Samantha wanted spending money. She went to a clothing store at the mall. And she applied for a job. Samantha is a Muslim. She wore a headscarf in her interview. Many Muslim women wear them. It's called a *hijab*.

The company refused to hire the teen. It said her scarf was against its dress code. Samantha said she didn't get the job because of her religion. She took the store to court. She said her civil rights were violated.

She won. The store had to pay her $20,000. They **appealed**. It asked another court to look at the case. This time Samantha lost. She then asked the U.S. Supreme

Court for help. The justices agreed with Samantha. They said the store treated her unfairly. The store violated her civil rights.

Think About It: *Did the civil rights movement bring about racial equality?*

[BEING CIVIL]

Civil rights are central to life in America. They protect us from unequal treatment.

It doesn't matter what color your skin is. What your religion is. Whether you're a boy or a girl. It doesn't matter if you are disabled. No one can treat you unfairly. You can sit where you want. Eat where you want. And work where you want.

Laws make it illegal to **discriminate**. Samantha said the store broke one of those laws. The Civil Rights Act of 1964. The law made it illegal not to hire a person because of their religion.

[RIGHT ON]

Civil rights protect us all no matter who you are. Many groups fought for their civil rights. African Americans, for one. Slavery ended after the Civil War. African Americans now had rights. Those rights needed protecting. Many people did not want to accept that their former slaves were their equals. Congress passed laws to make sure African Americans were treated fairly. It outlawed slavery. The 14th Amendment made former slaves citizens.

Some states ignored these laws. They passed new ones. Laws that made it legal to treat African

Americans unfairly. They were called Jim Crow laws. These laws kept whites and blacks apart. Blacks could not eat with whites. They had to ride in the back of buses. There were "colored only" restrooms. Even water fountains were separate.

Jim Crow stopped blacks from voting. It made getting an education hard. White children went to one school. Black children went to another school. White schools had more money and books.

African Americans wanted to be treated fairly. They protested. They forced Congress to pass more laws. These laws protected their civil rights. African American students could go to school where they wanted. They could sit in the front of the bus. Restaurants had to serve everyone. States could no longer stop African Americans from voting. African Americans made it easier for others to fight for their rights.

Other groups fought for their civil rights too. People fought to marry regardless of sexual orientation. In 2015, the Supreme Court said okay.

State laws also protect civil rights. It is illegal in many states to discriminate against homosexuals. They can live and work where they want. Gays and lesbians can use government services. But some states don't give them such protection.

ON THE JOB

It was 1954. Earl Warren was the chief justice of the Supreme Court. A case came before the court. ***Brown v. Board of Education***. Linda Brown was African American. She was in third grade. There was an all-white school close to her house. She tried to go there. The school refused to let her in. Her parents sued.

Warren thought black students should have the same rights as white students. He wanted to unite the schools. Separate schools were not equal, he said. He worked hard to get all the justices to agree. They did. That's why today people can go to the same schools regardless of skin color.

[CIVIL ACTIONS]

Civil liberties are important too. They are basic rights. Some are spelled out in the Bill of Rights. They include: freedoms of speech, press, and religion. The government cannot take them away. Sometimes it tries to reduce them. That's what some say happened. It was 2001. Terrorists flew planes into the World Trade Center.

FACES IN THE CROWD

Ernesto Miranda
Born: March 9, 1941
Died: January 31, 1976

"You have the right to remain silent ..." You hear it on TV and in the movies. It's what the police must say when they make an arrest. It wasn't always so. Police never used to tell people what their rights were. Then Ernesto Miranda came along.

The police in Phoenix, Arizona, knew Miranda well. He was a criminal. Even when he was a boy. He spent time in juvenile detention. In 1963, police arrested him. They said he committed a crime. They questioned him for two hours. Miranda confessed.

Police never told him he could talk to a lawyer. He didn't have to say a word. A jury sent him to jail. The Supreme Court threw out the conviction. Now all suspects have to be read their rights.

Congress wanted to stop more attacks. It passed the Patriot Act. The law did many things. It let the government collect phone records. Many said this was illegal. The case went to court. One court agreed. It said collecting phone records violated American civil liberties. It wasn't the final word on the law. Other courts took up the case too. Security is still on people's minds. But the Patriot Act expired. The USA Freedom Act replaced it. This act has restored some privacy rights.

➤ HISTORY HAPPENED HERE

Event: The Constitutional Convention

Where: Philadelphia, Pennsylvania

When: May 25–September 17, 1787

The writers of the Constitution had a long memory. They didn't like how the English treated them. They jailed Americans without just cause. Homes were searched without a warrant. The Constitution gives rights to those accused of a crime. They include the right

- to face a person's accuser.
- to a speedy trial.
- to a fair trial.
- to have a lawyer represent them.
- to have a trial by jury.
- to be free of cruel punishment.

You have certain rights. That doesn't mean you can do whatever you want. You have a right to speak freely. But you can't shout "Fire!" in a movie theater. You can worship in any church. But you don't have a right to kill in the name of religion. You can protest. But you can't start a riot.

Chapter 4
BIG GOVERNMENT

Hurricane Sandy was strong. The storm blew across the East Coast in 2012. It banged up several states. Its winds blew hard. They were nearly 115 miles per hour. Rain poured. Rivers rose. The Atlantic Ocean's waves hit the coast. Water flooded homes and roads. It caused billions of dollars in damage.

The storm was a killer. Many people died in the U.S. Homes were destroyed. People were tired. They were scared. Victims needed help.

Help was on the way. The Federal Emergency Management Agency (FEMA) stepped in. It is an agency within the Department of Homeland Security. It found people shelter. Gave them food. Helped them rebuild.

FEMA helps people after disasters. It is part of our government. There are many agencies. Some call it big government. Others call it the **bureaucracy**. Work is divided. Each department has a job to do. The bureaucracy enforces laws and rules. It collects taxes. Sends out checks. Works for the public good. And protects the nation. It keeps the economy strong.

[RESPONSIBILITY OF GOVERNING]

Congress can create government agencies. The Constitution gives them this power. In 1789, Congress created the Department of State. It helps the president with foreign affairs. Since then, Congress has created hundreds of agencies.

The federal bureaucracy is run by the executive branch. But it's Congress who creates most of these agencies.

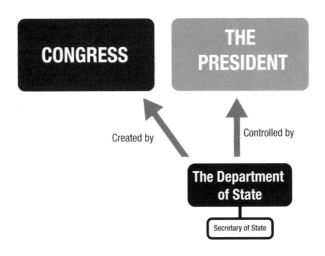

[WHO'S THE BOSS?]

The president runs federal agencies. Most of them anyway. Congress pays its bills. The agencies must answer to Congress. Congress makes sure they do their job. There are about 2.7 million workers. That does not include the military.

Some work for major departments. These are run by cabinet secretaries. The secretary of state runs the Department of State. Others work for government corporations. The U.S. Postal Service is one. The Federal Deposit Insurance Corporation (FDIC) is another. Some work only for the president. The Central Intelligence Agency (CIA) is one of them. The CIA is a spy agency.

Congress has small agencies too. The Library of Congress is one. The Government Accountability Office is another.

[CIVIL SERVANTS]

Government workers have a name. Bureaucrats. They aren't elected. The president can pick some. They could be friends. Or political **allies**. Some are business leaders or college teachers.

Most are **civil servants**. They are hired for their skill and knowledge. Employees do many jobs. Some are lawyers. Others

ON THE JOB

Some government jobs are for the dogs. Really! A dog musher works in Alaska. The person takes care of many dogs. The dogs live at Denali National Park. The worker takes the dogs out mushing in the snow.

are spies. Some are accountants. Others are clerks and scientists. Rules make it hard to fire government employees. That's to protect them against lawmakers. They can't fire a government worker. Not even if they disagree. But the rules go both ways. It makes it hard to fire a person who isn't doing their job.

[FOLLOWING THE RULES]

Some officials make rules. Officials in the Environmental Protection Agency (EPA), for example. The EPA sets levels for clean air and water. The rules are like

laws. Congress can review the rules. It can change them. Rules affect groups of people. Some are unpopular. Groups can sue the government to get rules changed.

Some agencies act like courts. Like the U.S.

Equal Employment Opportunity Commission
(EEOC). They protect job hunters against
discrimination. The EEOC tries to settle disputes.
They can also file lawsuits.

There is a list of government rules. It is in the
Federal Register. The *Register* was 2,600 pages long
80 years ago. In 2013, it was nearly 80,000 pages.
The page count is different every year.

Many say big government doesn't work. It is

wasteful. Service is bad. It is too big. Some say private firms should take over some jobs.

Sometimes the government gives away jobs. They hire private firms to do the work.

The government can do some jobs better, though. Like running the army. Presidents have tried to change the bureaucracy. Cut the size of government. Make rules simpler. It's easier said than done.

FACES IN THE CROWD

J. Edgar Hoover
Born: January 1, 1895
Died: May 2, 1972

J. Edgar Hoover loved secrets. Finding them was his job. He ran the FBI. Hoover was one of the most powerful officials in U.S. history. He worked for eight presidents. Hoover tricked people. Lied. And broke the law. The FBI director found out many things. Those secrets made him powerful. Presidents were afraid to fire him.

JAMES A. GARFIELD
REPUBLICAN CANDIDATE FOR PRESIDENT

CHESTER A. ARTHUR
REPUBLICAN CANDIDATE FOR VICE PRESIDENT

➤ HISTORY HAPPENED HERE

What: The Pendleton Act

When: January 16, 1883

Friends help friends get hired. Sounds fair. But it isn't. That's how people used to get government jobs. It was known as the spoils system. The winning political party rewarded supporters. A man killed President James Garfield. He had asked for a job. But he wasn't hired.

Vice President Chester Arthur became the new president. He wanted Congress to pass civil service reform. Senator George Pendleton of Ohio backed the bill. The law killed the spoils system. People got jobs based on skills. Not by who they knew. Or what party they voted for.

CHANGE
WE NEED

WWW.BARACKOBAMA.COM

Chapter 5
ELECTIONS

Gertrude Baines lived in a nursing home. She was 114. That didn't stop her from voting. "Miss Baines. This is the actual ballot," a worker said. She took Gertrude by the hand that held a pen. Gertrude filled in a circle. She voted for Barack Obama. He would win. The nation's first black president.

"Who did you vote for today?" someone asked. "Can you say his name?"

"Barack Obama," said Gertrude.

It was a big moment. Gertrude's grandparents were slaves. They could not vote. In 2008, Gertrude did. She was the oldest African American to vote for president. She died a year later. She was 115.

Gertrude wanted to vote. It was important. Voting is how we pick our leaders. Candidates run for office. People vote for the one they like. The one with the  most votes wins. Sounds simple. Right? Yes and no. Lots of things impact elections.

Think About It: *Is voting your civic duty? Are you a bad citizen if you don't vote?*

[PARTY ANIMALS]

Political parties are groups of people. They have the same ideas. Working together, they can win elections. Parties face-off on Election Day. Each wants to win. Be in charge. They want people to follow their views.

Parties pick candidates. Raise money. Hold rallies. Parties are as old as the nation. George Washington didn't like them. He said they were bad. They could hurt the country. No one listened to him. Political groups did well. They grew as the nation grew.

[THREE'S COMPANY]

Most people today are Democrats or Republicans. They are the two main parties. But they are not the only ones around. People join third parties. These parties offer other ways to solve problems.

Third parties can be powerful. They can change the way things are done. Sometimes voters like what third parties say. People force the two major parties to change their points of view.

[ELECTORAL COLLEGE]

The biggest election in the U.S. is for president. Yet we don't really vote for president. It's strange but true. We vote for electors. They are part of the Electoral College. It's not a real college. It is a group of people. *They* pick the president.

Each state has electors. How many? It depends on their numbers in Congress. The number in the Senate. Plus the number in the House. That's how many electors there are in each state. Large states like California have many electors. It has 55. Small states like Vermont do not have many at all. It has three. Those numbers are set until the next census. A census counts the population. It takes place every 10 years.

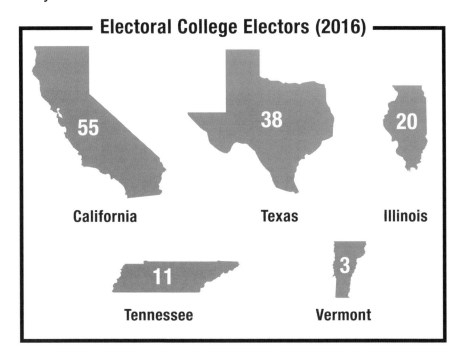

Electoral College Electors (2016)

California 55

Texas 38

Illinois 20

Tennessee 11

Vermont 3

The Electoral College has 538 electors. When the election is over, they get to work. They meet in each state. They cast their vote for president. A candidate who wins the popular vote in a state wins that state's electors. A candidate must earn a majority of electors. Only then will he or she become president. That number is 270.

You can read it in the Constitution. Some thought Congress should pick the president. Others thought it should be the people. The Electoral College was a **compromise**.

Some say the way we pick our president is unfair.

A person can win the most votes and still lose. It has happened four times in American history. But that's how the Electoral College works.

[TYPES OF ELECTIONS]

There are three types of elections: general, primary, and special. General elections are a two-step process. First there's a primary election. It reduces the number of candidates. Each party will have one candidate after the primary. The general

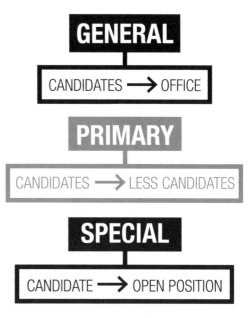

GENERAL

CANDIDATES ⟶ OFFICE

PRIMARY

CANDIDATES ⟶ LESS CANDIDATES

SPECIAL

CANDIDATE ⟶ OPEN POSITION

election is between those two candidates. A special election is usually held to fill an opening. An office may need to be filled between elections. A position may be open because of death, removal from office, or a resignation.

[ELECTION DAY]

Most people were farmers in the 18th century. Elections usually took place after the harvest. In 1792, state elections were held before the first Wednesday in December. There was a 34-day window before that date. So states could not hold elections whenever they felt like it. Most states held them in November. But each state decided on its own voting day.

In 1845, Congress decided that presidential elections would be held the first Tuesday after the first Monday in November. Monday was out. Some polls were far away. This would mean voters would have to travel on Sunday. Sunday was the day for church. Wednesday was not an option. That was market day for farmers. They would not be able to vote.

ON THE JOB

Electors can vote anyway they wish. But they almost never do. They are committed to their party's candidate.

[YOUR VOTE]

Is voting our most important right? Many think so.

There are countries where people cannot vote. They have no say in how their country should work. In the U.S. voters can share their  opinions. They do this by voting. People have a say in who helps make laws.

All U.S. citizens 18 or older have the right to vote, from local to national elections. People give up their chance to make a difference if they don't vote.

➤ HISTORY HAPPENED HERE

Event: Election of 1800

What: A Tie for President

Elections can end in a tie. That's not a secret. The election of 1800 ended that way. It was between Thomas Jefferson and Aaron Burr. They were two founding fathers. Each had the same number of electoral votes. But there was a problem. Jefferson was running for president. Burr for vice president. The writers of the Constitution never considered a tie like this. The election went to the House of Representatives. It picked Thomas Jefferson. The 12th Amendment fixed the problem.

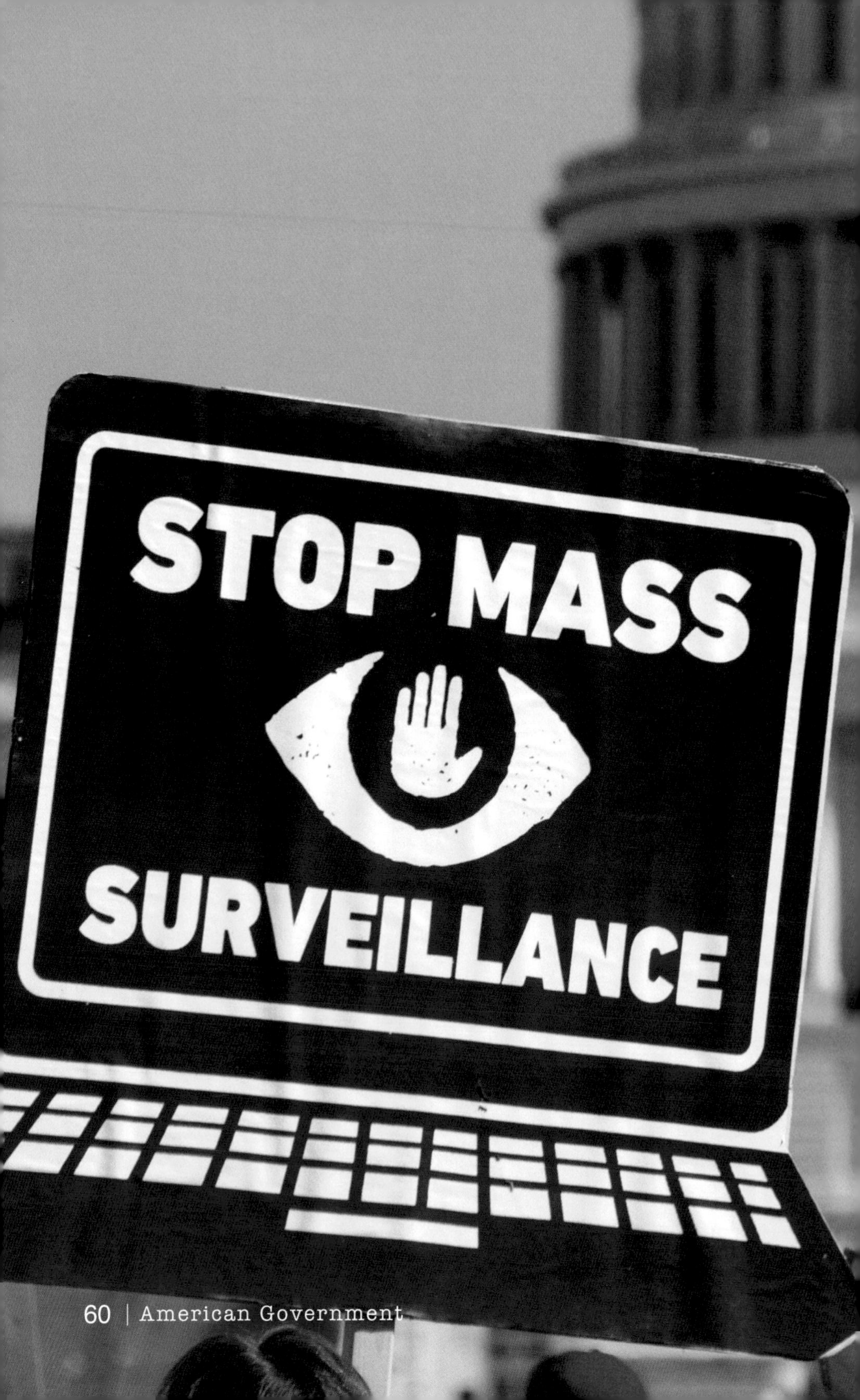
STOP MASS
SURVEILLANCE

Chapter 6
WE THE PEOPLE

Edward Snowden went to work each day. He worked for the government at the National Security Agency (NSA). Its job is to protect the country. Snowden had a computer. He could read many things. He saw how the NSA did its job. He was upset. The NSA was spying on Americans. Snowden thought the government was breaking the law. He said the U.S. was violating our civil rights.

Snowden made a decision. In 2013, he stole what he read. Thousands of pages of secrets. He left the U.S. The documents were **leaked** to the press. Reporters let the public know what the NSA was up to.

We learned many things. The NSA looked at who people called. It spied on foreign leaders. The agency looked at what people were searching for online. It had a team of hackers. They broke into computer systems.

People were shocked. They demanded investigations. Some said Snowden was a criminal. He was a traitor who stole secrets. The government wanted to arrest him. Others said he was a patriot. A **whistle-blower**. A person who tattled on the government. Snowden got people talking. He forced the NSA to change.

Think About It: *What does it mean to be a good citizen? Was Edward Snowden a good citizen? What about Daniel Ellsberg?*

[ROLES TO PLAY]

In the U.S. the president has a role to play. So does Congress. Judges and bureaucrats also have a role to play. So do we, the citizens. We have the biggest job of all.

Event: The Pentagon Papers

Where: Washington, D.C.

When: June 13, 1971, in the *New York Times*

Should we question the government? It's our duty. Daniel Ellsberg did it. He protested the Vietnam War. The war began in the 1960s. Ellsberg worked for the Department of Defense. He helped write a report. It showed what U.S. officials were thinking at the time. The war could never be won. Officials lied to the nation.

Ellsberg got mad. He copied the papers. They were given to a reporter. A newspaper printed a series of articles. That changed the public's opinion about the government. It was the beginning of the end of the Nixon Administration.

President Nixon thought Ellsberg knew more secrets. He tried to discredit Ellsberg. The president put together a secret team. They broke the law. The team listened to Ellsberg's phone calls. And they broke into his doctor's office. Those same men broke into the Watergate complex in 1972. Nixon resigned in 1974.

People are the real power. Not the president. Not senators. Not judges or mayors. We tell all those lawmakers what to do. Citizens have many responsibilities.

[STAYING INFORMED]

Keeping up on issues. It allows us to run our country, state, and city. We need to know about laws. And about what the government is doing. Speaking our mind is also very important. We might not like what the government does. We can write a letter to the editor. Blog. Protest. Speaking up is a way to tell our representatives what to do.

STAY INFORMED & GET INVOLVED

FACES IN THE CROWD
Kid Activists

Speaking up! Standing up! Trying to change policy. That's an important thing for people to do. That's what 40 children tried to do in 2013. They came from all over the country. They were part of a national youth group. They fought for the rights of immigrants. They came to the U.S. Capitol to talk to lawmakers. They wanted immigration rules to change.

The children sang songs. Asked questions. Gave out holiday cards. They wanted lawmakers to pass an immigration reform bill. Some lawmakers ignored them. Police said they would arrest the children. Some kids cried. But they stayed. They made their point.

[VOTING]

All Americans that can vote should. Your vote can make a difference. Honest! George W. Bush won Florida by 537 votes. Harry S. Truman won the 1948 election by just one vote per precinct in California and Ohio.

In 1997, a state representative from Vermont lost by one vote. In 1989, a school district proposition in Lansing, Michigan, failed because of a tie. In 1994, a state representative from Wyoming tied for his seat with his opponent. The tie was settled by the governor. He drew the winning name from a cowboy hat. The winner's name was written on a Ping-Pong ball.

Voting is at the heart of democracy. Voting sends a message. It tells the government how we want to be ruled. Yet less than half of eligible voters do vote. Why is that? Are we just lazy citizens?

There are many reasons people don't vote. Some don't care. They don't think government works. They believe their vote doesn't matter. Some say voting takes too long. Others are too busy.

It is hard to vote in many places. It's tough to sign up. Hard to get to the polls. Elections are held during the week. People can't get off work to vote.

[RESPECTING LAWS AND PEOPLE]

All sorts of people live in the U.S. Different races. Religions. Cultures. Yet we share certain things. Certain values. Laws.

Following them is our duty. A good citizen respects the beliefs and rights of others. That respect protects all our liberties.

[PAYING TAXES]

Who likes paying taxes? Few do. Yet taxes are important. It allows the government to do things for us. It pays for schools. Keeps our country safe. Makes sick people well. Provides food for the poor. And helps people when disaster strikes.

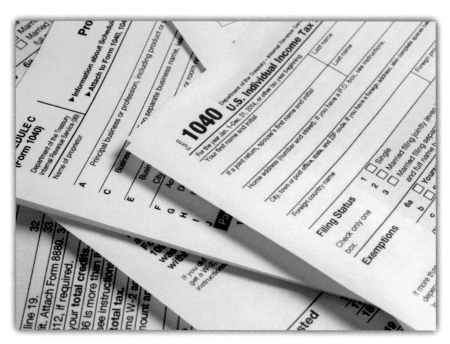

[SERVING ON A JURY]

Everyone has the right to a fair trial. And a speedy trial too. A person also has the right to be tried by people just like them. A jury.  Juries protect the rights of the accused. It makes sure trials are just. Juries help a person get fair treatment.

[DEFENDING THE COUNTRY]

Wars happen. Sometimes people fight to defend the U.S. The military is made up of volunteers. However, Congress could set up a draft. A draft means that a person *has* to serve in the armed forces. Being a soldier isn't the only way to defend the U.S. There are other ways. Thousands of civilians work for the military. Some worked in war zones like Iraq and Afghanistan.

[FOR THE PEOPLE]

Government of the people. By the people. For the people. That's America. That's how George Washington saw it. Benjamin Franklin. Roger Sherman. James Madison. All the Constitution's **framers**.

Democracy is not perfect. It's messy and difficult. People argue. They scream at each other. There are winners and losers. It was true in 1787. It's true today.

The ultimate rulers of our democracy are not a president and senators and congressmen and government officials, but the voters of this country.

—Franklin D. Roosevelt

GLOSSARY

allies: people that join together for a common reason

Anti-Federalist: Americans who opposed the Constitution in the late 1700s

appealed: request to a higher court to reverse a lower court decision

bicameral: lawmaking group with two houses or chambers

bureaucracy: the many agencies, sub-agencies, and workers within government

civil servants: an employee in a government agency

compromise: when two sides make a deal but neither "wins"

constitutional representative democracy: nation with a constitution where citizens vote for representatives who make the decisions

delegates: person(s) authorized to represent another

direct democracy: all citizens vote on every issue; majority rules

discriminate: treat unfairly or unjustly

federal republic: a form of government where the central government shares power with its states

framers: people who wrote the U.S. Constitution

implied: suggested or understood but not directly stated

interpret: to tell or explain the meaning of

leaked: the unofficial release of secrets, usually to the media

pardon: forgive a person convicted of a crime and restore legal rights

ratify: to make official by voting for it

veto: to refuse or reject something, like a new law

whistle-blower: person who exposes illegal acts

PRIMARY SOURCES
[A LOOK AT THE PAST]

What is a primary source? It is a document. Or a piece of art. Or an artifact. It was created in the past. A primary source can answer questions. It can also lead to more questions. Three primary sources are included in this book. **The Preamble to the U.S. Constitution**. It explains why the framers chose to create a republic. **The Bill of Rights**. It guarantees certain freedoms. And the **Declaration of Independence**. It stresses natural rights. More can be found at the National Archives (online at *archives.gov.*) These sources were written for the people. (That means us.) The people broke free from the king's tyranny. The United States of America was born. Read the primary sources. Be an eyewitness to history.

We the people of the United States, in order to form a more perfect Union, establish justice, insure domestic Tranquility, provide for the common defense, promote the general welfare, and secure the blessings of liberty to ourselves and our posterity, do ordain and establish this Constitution for the United States of America.

[PREAMBLE]

THE U.S. BILL OF RIGHTS

THE PREAMBLE TO THE BILL OF RIGHTS

CONGRESS OF THE UNITED STATES begun and held at the City of New York, Wednesday, March 4, 1789.

THE Conventions of a number of the states, having at the time of their adopting the Constitution, expressed a desire, in order to prevent misconstruction or abuse of its powers, that further declaratory and restrictive clauses should be added: And as extending the ground of public confidence in the government, will best ensure the beneficent ends of its institution.

RESOLVED by the Senate and House of Representatives

of the United States of America, in Congress assembled,

two-thirds of both Houses concurring, that the following

Articles be proposed to the legislatures of the several

states, as amendments to the Constitution of the United

States, all, or any of which articles, when ratified by three-

fourths of the said legislatures, to be valid to all intents

and purposes, as part of the said Constitution; viz.

ARTICLES in addition to, and amendment of the Constitution

of the United States of America, proposed by Congress, and

ratified by the legislatures of the several states, pursuant to

the fifth article of the original Constitution.

AMENDMENT I

Congress shall make no law respecting an establishment of religion, or prohibiting the free exercise thereof; or abridging the freedom of speech, or of the press; or the right of the people peaceably to assemble, and to petition the government for a redress of grievances.

AMENDMENT II

A well regulated militia, being necessary to the security of a free state, the right of the people to keep and bear arms, shall not be infringed.

AMENDMENT III

No soldier shall, in time of peace be quartered in any house, without the consent of the owner, nor in time of war, but in a manner to be prescribed by law.

AMENDMENT IV

The right of the people to be secure in their persons, houses, papers, and effects, against unreasonable searches and seizures, shall not be violated, and no warrants shall issue, but upon probable cause, supported by oath or affirmation, and particularly describing the place to be searched, and the persons or things to be seized.

AMENDMENT V

No person shall be held to answer for a capital, or otherwise infamous crime, unless on a presentment or indictment of a grand jury, except in cases arising in the land or naval forces, or in the militia, when in actual service in time of war or public danger; nor shall any person be subject for the same offense to be twice put in jeopardy of life or limb; nor shall be compelled in any criminal case to be a witness against himself, nor be deprived of life, liberty, or property, without due process of law; nor shall private property be taken for public use, without just compensation.

AMENDMENT VI

In all criminal prosecutions, the accused shall enjoy the right to a speedy and public trial, by an impartial jury of the state and district wherein the crime shall have been committed, which district shall have been previously ascertained by law, and to be informed of the nature and cause of the accusation; to be confronted with the witnesses against him; to have compulsory process for obtaining witnesses in his favor, and to have the assistance of counsel for his defense.

AMENDMENT VII

In suits at common law, where the value in controversy shall exceed 20 dollars, the right of trial by jury shall be preserved, and no fact tried by a jury, shall be otherwise re-examined in any court of the United States, than according to the rules of the common law.

AMENDMENT VIII

Excessive bail shall not be required, nor excessive fines imposed, nor cruel and unusual punishments inflicted.

AMENDMENT IX

The enumeration in the Constitution, of certain rights, shall not be construed to deny or disparage others retained by the people.

AMENDMENT X

The powers not delegated to the United States by the Constitution, nor prohibited by it to the states, are reserved to the states respectively, or to the people.

IN CONGRESS, JULY 4, 1776.

The unanimous Declaration of the thirteen United States of America,

When in the course of human events, it becomes necessary for one people to dissolve the political bands which have connected them with another, and to assume among the powers of the earth, the separate and equal station to which the laws of nature and of nature's god entitle them, a decent respect to the opinions of mankind requires that they should declare the causes which impel them to the separation.

❧❦

We hold these truths to be self-evident, that all men are created equal, that they are endowed by their Creator with certain unalienable rights, that among these are life, liberty and the pursuit of happiness. That to secure these rights, governments are instituted among men, deriving their just powers from the consent of the governed. That whenever any form of government becomes destructive of these ends, it is the right of the people to alter or to abolish it, and to institute new government, laying its foundation on such principles and organizing its powers in such form, as to them shall seem most likely to effect their safety and happiness. Prudence, indeed, will dictate that governments long established should not be changed for light and transient causes; and accordingly all experience has shown, that mankind are more disposed to suffer, while evils are sufferable, than to right themselves by abolishing the forms to which they are accustomed. But when a long train of abuses and usurpations, pursuing invariably the same object evinces a design to reduce them under absolute despotism, it is their right, it is their duty, to throw off such government, and to provide new guards for their future security. Such has been the patient sufferance of these colonies; and such is now the necessity which constrains them to alter their former systems of government. The history of the present king of Great Britain is a history of repeated injuries and usurpations, all having in direct object the establishment of an absolute tyranny over these states. To prove this, let facts be submitted to a candid world.

He has refused his assent to laws, the most wholesome and necessary for the public good.

He has forbidden his governors to pass laws of immediate and pressing importance, unless suspended in their operation till his assent should be obtained; and when so suspended, he has utterly neglected to attend to them.

He has refused to pass other laws for the accommodation of large districts of people, unless those people would relinquish the right of representation in the legislature, a right inestimable to them and formidable to tyrants only.

He has called together legislative bodies at places unusual, uncomfortable, and distant from the depository of their public records, for the sole purpose of fatiguing them into compliance with his measures.

He has dissolved representative houses repeatedly, for opposing with manly firmness his invasions on the rights of the people.

He has refused for a long time, after such dissolutions, to cause others to be elected; whereby the legislative powers, incapable of annihilation, have returned to the people at large for their exercise; the state remaining in the mean time exposed to all the dangers of invasion from without, and convulsions within.

He has endeavored to prevent the population of these states; for that purpose obstructing the laws for naturalization of foreigners; refusing to pass others to encourage their migrations hither, and raising the conditions of new appropriations of lands.

He has obstructed the administration of justice, by refusing his assent to laws for establishing judiciary powers.

He has made judges dependent on his will alone, for the tenure of their offices, and the amount and payment of their salaries.

He has erected a multitude of new offices, and sent hither swarms of officers to harrass our people, and eat out their substance.

He has kept among us, in times of peace, standing armies without the consent of our legislatures.

He has affected to render the military independent of and superior to the civil power.

He has combined with others to subject us to a jurisdiction foreign to our constitution, and unacknowledged by our laws; giving his assent to their acts of pretended legislation:

For quartering large bodies of armed troops among us;

For protecting them, by a mock trial, from punishment for any murders which they should commit on the inhabitants of these states;

For cutting off our trade with all parts of the world;

For imposing taxes on us without our consent;

For depriving us in many cases, of the benefits of trial by jury;

For transporting us beyond seas to be tried for pretended offenses;

For abolishing the free system of English laws in a neighboring province, establishing therein an arbitrary government, and enlarging its boundaries so as to render it at once an example and fit instrument for introducing the same absolute rule into these colonies;

For taking away our charters, abolishing our most valuable laws, and altering fundamentally the forms of our governments;

For suspending our own legislatures, and declaring themselves invested with power to legislate for us in all cases whatsoever.

He has abdicated government here, by declaring us out of his protection and waging war against us.

He has plundered our seas, ravaged our coasts, burnt our towns, and destroyed the lives of our people.

He is at this time transporting large armies of foreign mercenaries to complete the works of death, desolation and tyranny, already begun with circumstances of cruelty and perfidy scarcely paralleled in the most barbarous ages, and totally unworthy the head of a civilized nation.

He has constrained our fellow citizens taken captive on the high seas to bear arms against their country, to become the executioners of their friends and brethren, or to fall themselves by their hands.

He has excited domestic insurrections amongst us, and has endeavored to bring on the inhabitants of our frontiers, the merciless Indian savages, whose known rule of warfare, is an undistinguished destruction of all ages, sexes and conditions.

[DECLARATION OF INDEPENDENCE]

In every stage of these oppressions we have petitioned for redress in the most humble terms: our repeated petitions have been answered only by repeated injury. A prince whose character is thus marked by every act which may define a tyrant, is unfit to be the ruler of a free people.

Nor have we been wanting in attentions to our Brittish brethren. We have warned them from time to time of attempts by their legislature to extend an unwarrantable jurisdiction over us. We have reminded them of the circumstances of our emigration and settlement here. We have appealed to their native justice and magnanimity, and we have conjured them by the ties of our common kindred to disavow these usurpations, which, would inevitably interrupt our connections and correspondence. They too have been deaf to the voice of justice and of consanguinity. We must, therefore, acquiesce in the necessity, which denounces our separation, and hold them, as we hold the rest of mankind, enemies in war, in peace friends.

We, therefore, the representatives of the United States of America, in General Congress, assembled, appealing to the Supreme Judge of the world for the rectitude of our intentions, do, in the name, and by authority of the good people of these colonies, solemnly publish and declare, that these united colonies are, and of right ought to be free and independent states; that they are absolved from all allegiance to the British Crown, and that all political connection between them and the state of Great Britain, is and ought to be totally dissolved; and that as free and independent states, they have full power to levy war, conclude peace, contract alliances, establish commerce, and to do all other acts and things which independent states may of right do. And for the support of this declaration, with a firm reliance on the protection of divine providence, we mutually pledge to each other our lives, our fortunes and our sacred honor.

There are 56 signatures on the Declaration. They appear in six columns.

COLUMN 1

GEORGIA

Button Gwinnett

Lyman Hall

George Walton

COLUMN 2

NORTH CAROLINA

William Hooper

Joseph Hewes

John Penn

SOUTH CAROLINA

Edward Rutledge

Thomas Heyward, Jr.

Thomas Lynch, Jr.

Arthur Middleton

COLUMN 3

MASSACHUSETTS

John Hancock

MARYLAND

Samuel Chase

William Paca

Thomas Stone

Charles Carroll of Carrollton

VIRGINIA

George Wythe

Richard Henry Lee

Thomas Jefferson

Benjamin Harrison

Thomas Nelson, Jr.

Francis Lightfoot Lee

Carter Braxton

COLUMN 4

PENNSYLVANIA

Robert Morris

Benjamin Rush

Benjamin Franklin

John Morton

George Clymer

James Smith

George Taylor

James Wilson

George Ross

DELAWARE

Caesar Rodney

George Read

Thomas McKean

COLUMN 5

NEW YORK

William Floyd

Philip Livingston

Francis Lewis

Lewis Morris

NEW JERSEY

Richard Stockton

John Witherspoon

Francis Hopkinson

John Hart

Abraham Clark

COLUMN 6

NEW HAMPSHIRE

Josiah Bartlett

William Whipple

MASSACHUSETTS

Samuel Adams

John Adams

Robert Treat Paine

Elbridge Gerry

RHODE ISLAND

Stephen Hopkins

William Ellery

CONNECTICUT

Roger Sherman

Samuel Huntington

William Williams

Oliver Wolcott

NEW HAMPSHIRE

Matthew Thornton

[DECLARATION OF INDEPENDENCE]

Be an engaged citizen in today's world.
Meet life's challenges after high school. Are
you fully prepared for democratic decision
making? Do you know how to address
and approach issues in a democratic
and responsible way? These five unique
handbooks will show you how.

AMERICAN GOVERNMENT

American Government
FOUNDATIONS

John Perritano

9781680211184

American Government
OFFICE OF THE PRESIDENT

John Perritano

9781680211214

American Government
CONGRESS

John Perritano

9781680211207

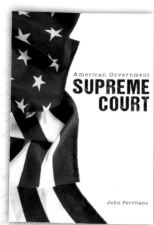

American Government
SUPREME COURT

John Perritano

9781680211191

American Government
POLITICAL PARTIES

John Perritano

9781680211221